ON THE RUN

ON THE RUN

By ERIC DICKERSON
with Steve Delsohn

CONTEMPORARY
BOOKS, INC.
CHICAGO • NEW YORK

Library of Congress Cataloging-in-Publication Data

Dickerson, Eric, 1960–
  On the run.

  1. Dickerson, Eric, 1960–   2. Football players
United States—Biography.   I. Delsohn, Steve.
II. Title.
GV939.D52A3   1986   796.332'092'4 [B]   86-13445
ISBN 0-8092-4973-1

Copyright © 1986 by Eric Dickerson and Steve Delsohn
All rights reserved
Published by Contemporary Books, Inc.
180 North Michigan Avenue, Chicago, Illinois 60601
Manufactured in the United States of America
Library of Congress Catalog Card Number: 86-13445
International Standard Book Number: 0-8092-4973-1

Published simultaneously in Canada by Beaverbooks, Ltd.
195 Allstate Parkway, Valleywood Business Park
Markham, Ontario L3R 4T8 Canada

To my mother, Viola Dickerson, whose inspiration and support have meant everything to me

CONTENTS

ACKNOWLEDGMENTS ix
1 A SOLID FOUNDATION 1
2 GROWING PAINS 17
3 COLLEGE KID 31
4 WELCOME TO THE PROS 45
5 CLOSING IN ON O.J. 71
6 ONE WIN FROM THE SUPER BOWL 99

ACKNOWLEDGMENTS

Special thanks to Georgia Frontiere, John Robinson, the entire Rams Organization, and all my teammates past and present, especially offensive players Bill Bain, Russ Bolinger, Dieter Brock, Ron Brown, Henry Ellard, Vince Ferragamo, Mike Guman, Dennis Harrah, Kent Hill, Jeff Kemp, Irv Pankey, Barry Redden, Joe Shearin, Jackie Slater, Tony Slaton, and Doug Smith.

ON THE RUN

1
A SOLID FOUNDATION

When I was a kid I wasn't exactly Mr. Cool.

For starters I was terribly shy around girls. I liked them and everything, it's just that I was never real relaxed when I got around them. I would go to say something clever, and my mouth wouldn't cooperate with my brain. So mostly I'd stand around and smile a lot.

When I was 15, there was a girl in my neighborhood named Lisa. She was cute and I was crazy about her, but like any other girl she made me nervous. Lisa was at my house one day and it was time for her to leave.

"You going to walk me outside?" she asked.

My heart started doing the 100-yard dash. I could see in her eyes what she wanted, and I wasn't quite sure I was ready for it. I mean, I'd never kissed a girl before in my life. When she asked me, again, to walk her outside, I was ready with a brilliant comeback.

"For what?"

"Come on, Eric, just come on outside."

"What's outside?"
"Walk me outside!!"
"OK, OK."

When we got outside we kissed. Then we kissed some more. Just for good measure we kissed good-bye. Maybe if I'd been more experienced I would have reacted with a little more cool. As it was, by the time we broke for air I was head over heels in love. And once I knew what kissing was all about, I couldn't get enough of it. Lisa and I kissed, I mean dated, for the next two years.

So now the truth is out: when I was little I was never some kind of Romeo. But at least I was consistent. Because I also wasn't a tough guy.

Every town has its human punching bag. In Sealy, Texas, when I was a little kid, that was me. I was the guy the neighborhood bullies used to beat up when they wanted to make their reputations. Need to become a certified bully? Just jump all over Eric. I hated it with a passion. Being black I always liked. Being black and blue I could always do without.

Why did the local tough guys always feel the need to knock *me* around? I'm not exactly sure, but I guess I've got a few ideas:

- I still hadn't filled out, so my build wasn't exactly intimidating. Today I'm 6'3" and 220 pounds. But, boy, did it take a while. I was tall but painfully skinny when I was a kid. More like the "before" shot than the "after."
- I was also perceived as a momma's boy. I never understood this. So what if my mom went with me everywhere?
- From the time I was 12 years old I wore glasses. You know how much abuse kids who wear glasses get.
- As if I needed more problems, some of my friends thought my head was shaped funny. One of them told me it was shaped like an egg. He used to kid me all the time: if I ever played football I wouldn't even need a helmet; I could just wear a giant eggshell.

That's me with Viola, who's characteristically giving me a helping hand. Viola's my great-great aunt, who became my adoptive mother. She's always been there for me, and there's nothing I wouldn't do for her.

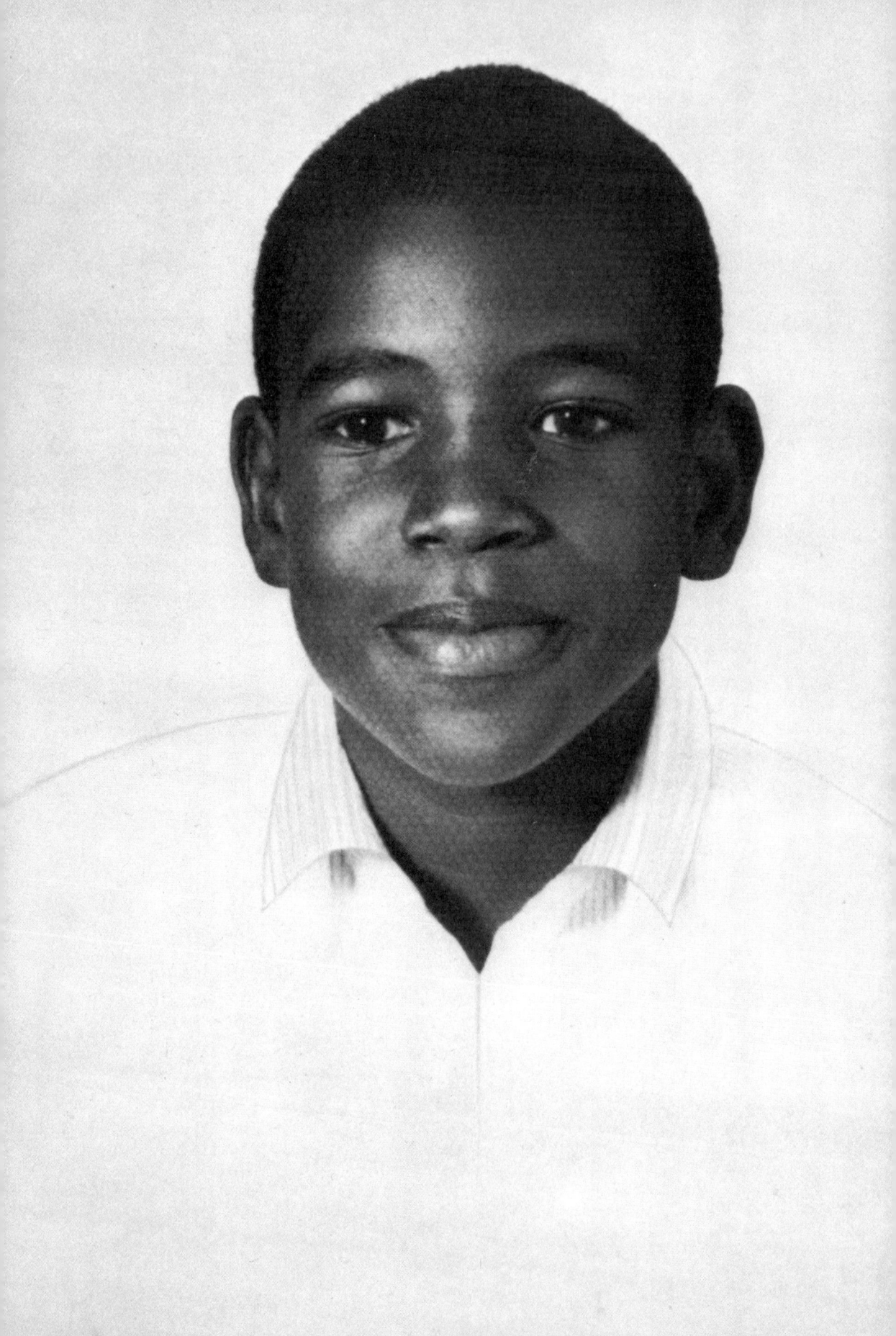

A Solid Foundation

I was a dreamer when I was a kid. Man, could I dream. That I could do as well as anyone.

Westview, a nearby neighborhood where one of my friends lived, used to get me dreaming all the time. It was where all the lawyers and doctors lived—the houses were large and airy, with expensive cars in every driveway. Whenever I visited my buddy, I was awed by the inside of his house. I'd wait for him in his living room, gawking at the rugs, the fireplace, the beautiful pictures. And I was always dreaming... "Some day, I'll have my own place just like this."

(Before I go on, this is a good time to set something straight: when I was a child my family was not dirt poor. True, we didn't walk around the house in designer bathrobes, but I always had clean clothes and I never went hungry. I'm not crazy about labels, but economically, I suppose you could say we were part of the lower-middle class. So were most of the people who lived in Sealy, Texas. It's a cattle and farming town, with a lot of people who have gone there to retire. Incomes are generally modest.)

I was the guy the neighborhood bullies used to beat up when they wanted to make their reputations. Need to become a certified bully? Just jump all over Eric. Being black I always liked. Being black and blue I could always do without.

Today I've realized my dream—I own my own big house. It's in Sealy and my mother Viola lives there. That house is something I'm extremely proud of. It sits on 4,000 square feet and it's one of the nicest houses in Sealy. That's exactly the way I wanted it.

There's nothing I wouldn't do to make my mother happy. Especially at this point in her life, it means a lot to me that my mom be comfortable. She's worked long and hard for so many years. Now should be her time to relax.

I was a happy child but a little on the shy side. My accomplishments in sports were good for my confidence.

When she was young my mom used to dream about going to college to become a school teacher. But it never happened. My mother's father was a sharecropper. He was very poor, and his wife and seven children all had to go to work on the family farm. The women worked as hard as the men. My mom milked cows and plowed the fields. She picked cotton by the bushel, earning about a dollar for every 100 pounds. They worked from sunup to sundown in that brutal Texas heat.

Without a doubt, my mom has been the greatest single influence on my life. Every time I've been faced with a major decision, I've made it a point to get my mother's input. I value my mom's opinion because I value her sense of what's important. She doesn't really know much about football—baseball's her favorite sport—but she does know a lot about life.

Some of my friends thought my head was shaped funny. One of them told me it was shaped like an egg. He used to kid me all the time, saying that if I ever played football I wouldn't even need a helmet; I could just wear a giant eggshell.

On the surface, my own life has clearly changed. I make a lot of money and I own a lot of nice things. But *inside*, I can honestly say that I still feel like the same old Eric—my values and my ethics are still intact. And it all comes back to the way my mother raised me. My mom had dozens of sayings when I was younger. Among others, one of them really stuck with me:

"Just as fast as you can go up, you can come down just as quickly."

To this day, I still believe that. And that belief has helped keep my success in its proper perspective. I love playing football, but I also know it's going to end some day. When I do retire I want to be known as more than a good football player. I want to be thought of as a quality person.

I told you I was a happy child.

My first year in the pros I bought Viola a satellite dish. It's great—now she watches all the Rams' games.

A Solid Foundation

Let me explain about my mom now. Viola, who I've referred to as my mother, is not my mother by birth. Viola is actually my great-great aunt, but she is my mother through adoption. Just as a man named Kary, who was Viola's husband before he passed away, was my father through adoption. My natural mother's name is Helen and my natural father's name is Richard. But Helen was only 17 years old when I was born. She and Richard weren't married, and they had no concrete plans for the future. Still so young herself, Helen felt Viola would be much better equipped to raise a baby. Viola agreed. When I was born, it was Viola who brought me home from Sealy Hospital. When I was three months old, it was Viola who adopted me. And it's Viola who I've always called Mom.

Viola never had any of her own children, but she lent a hand in raising some of her brothers' and sisters' children. That included Helen, my natural mother, who lived with Viola since she was 16 months old. As a result, Helen and I grew up in the same house together. In fact, for a long, long time, I thought that Helen was my sister, Viola was my natural mother, and Kary was my natural father. I didn't find out the entire story until I was 15 years old.

Viola, who I've referred to as my mother, is not my mother by birth. Viola is actually my great-great aunt, but she is my mother through adoption. My natural mother's name is Helen. But Helen was only 17 years old when I was born. In fact, for a long time, I thought Helen was my sister. I didn't find out the entire story until I was 15 years old.

It happened at school. I was talking with one of my favorite teachers when she told me that my father was in town. She said it matter of factly, because she thought I knew. I replied that of course my father was in town; Kary was always in town—he lived there.

"I mean your real father is in town," she said.

I still had no idea what she was talking about, and I asked her what she meant.

Then she told me. She said my real father's name was Richard. She didn't explain the rest because I didn't give her the chance. Before she went any further I ran right home and asked Viola.

"Mom," I asked her, "who is this guy Richard?"

First Viola looked stunned. Then she was furious.

"Who," she demanded, "told you about Richard?"

"My teacher did. Now who is this Richard guy?"

Viola sat me down and told me everything.

I know—you're wondering how I felt. I have to admit I was shocked. I mean, this was not small news. But I never felt crushed, not even close. To be perfectly honest, I wasn't even sad. I never cried, never considered running away. I just accepted it and went on living my life. It didn't change anything.

Under different circumstances, my reaction might have been different. Maybe if I didn't love Viola so much it would have bothered me more. But I thought she was the greatest person in the world.

Maybe if I'd never had the chance to meet my natural mother, I would be resentful. But Helen was living in the same house with me—I saw her every day. To this day, I still think of Helen as a sister. We can talk about anything together. She's married now and she lives right next to my mom. We're all family and we all love each other.

Besides all of that, there's another reason why I never got upset: because I always had a father. I really loved Kary. If I ever have my own children, I hope I can be half the father Kary was.

There's an old saying that opposites attract. It's gotta be true—otherwise my mother and my father never would have lasted. Viola was always feisty—she loved a good argument—but Kary was always so gentle. Viola would want to argue and Kary would just sit there and listen to her scream. But, just like me, my mother adored Kary.

A Solid Foundation

When I was in high school Kary loved to watch me play football. But Viola didn't want him going to watch at all because Kary had a history of heart problems. He used to have frequent chest pains and it would scare the hell out of all of us. My mom would constantly warn him: "You stop going to those games. You'll die in those stands one day watching Eric play football." But Kary always came anyway. The thing I used to love, he'd always arrive for an 8:00 P.M. game at 5:00 or 5:30. He didn't want to miss anything. He got a tremendous kick from watching his son play ball.

Kary was one of the deacons at our church and our home always had a powerful dose of religion. Kary used to come into my room at night and talk to me about God. One conversation I remember so vividly: Kary told me that someday we all had to die. And that one day he would die, and then we wouldn't be able to have these conversations. And, he said, I would miss him.

I was devastated when Kary died. On the day of his death I remembered what he had told me: that one day he'd pass on and we wouldn't be able to talk. And I realized that all along he'd been trying to prepare me, because he knew that he was ill. But when Kary died I wasn't prepared at all. Kary died nine years ago, when I was a junior in high school, but I still haven't gotten over it. Neither has my momma. Kary was a beautiful man.

As for Richard, my natural father, he lives in Houston. I don't see him much. When I do see him, I don't look at him as if he's my father. I look at him, I guess you could say, as I would a casual friend. What I mean is, there's no feeling of love for him, but there's also no bitterness. I know he's my natural father and I respect him. I like him. It's just that I hardly know him.

There is something about Richard that most people don't know. He was an excellent running back, first in high school and later at Prairie View College in Texas. Richard loves to tell me that he gave me my ability to run. I don't know about that, but maybe there is some similarity to our running styles.

A few years ago I was approached by one of the coaches of the

St. Louis Cardinals. He looked like he wanted to ask me something but was struggling to find the proper words.

"Can I ask you a question?" he finally asked me.

"Of course."

"I don't want to get too personal, but is your father Richard Seal?"

He caught me by surprise.

"Yes he is," I said. "But why do you ask me that?"

"I knew it, I knew it!"

"How did you know it?"

"Because I know Richard. You run just like him."

Saying that I had a sheltered childhood is like saying that the Super Bowl gets a lot of hype. It's true, but it's also a major understatement.

Part of that was thanks to my mother. She made me come straight home after school. At night I couldn't go to baseball or basketball games. It seemed like I couldn't go anywhere. I take that back. I could go anywhere I wanted—as long as my mother went with me.

It's not that my mom didn't trust me—she just wasn't sure about some of the other kids. She didn't want me running in a bad crowd, picking up their habits. She was especially concerned about marijuana. It was just becoming popular among kids and she was terrified that I would try it. But I never did. Not even once. First, I had no desire whatsoever; it just didn't interest me. The second reason, the same reason I rarely got into trouble when I was growing up, was simple: my mom could really sling a whip.

One of the worst whippings I ever got came when I was about 17. By then I was allowed to go out, but I still had to be home by 10:00 P.M. One night I came home at 12:30. After her arm got tired from whipping me, my mom gave me a lecture. She said there was no reason for me to be out that late, that nothing was even open. The next thing she told me I'll never forget.

A Solid Foundation 13

A couple of the girls in my life: my sisters Tasha and Lisa.

"Eric, the only thing open after 12 is legs."

At the time I blushed and blushed. Now when I think of it, it cracks me up.

When he was properly provoked, Kary could also administer a pretty sound whipping. Looking back, I think those whippings were good for me—the thought of another burning behind was all the incentive I needed to stay in line. Still, there was another reason I grew up gradually. I can explain it in two words: Sealy, Texas.

One night I came home at 12:30. After her arm got tired from whipping me, my mom gave me a lecture. She said there was no reason for me to be out that late: "Eric, the only thing open after 12 is legs."

Sealy, population roughly 4,000, is a town near Houston, mostly a place where people go to retire. For that it's perfect: peaceful, clean, and unhurried. But I was only a kid, and to me Sealy was about as exciting as folding laundry. I'll give you a perfect example of how boring Sealy was. When I was in high school our idea of a big night, really tearing it up, was hanging out at the local 7-Eleven. I think that says it all.

In my teens, Sealy's crawling pace drove me nuts. I remember telling people when I was in junior high school: "Once I leave this place, I'm never coming back except to visit my mother."

Chalk it up to youthful impatience. Because now, whenever I get a chance, I love going back to Sealy. I like Los Angeles, but sometimes the pace can get all too hectic. I'm a worrier by nature and sometimes I worry myself right into these rotten tension headaches. As soon as I get back to Sealy they always go right away. Going back to Sealy—where no one's in a rush, where they don't even lock their doors or windows—gives me a tremendous feeling of freedom.

A Solid Foundation

I've always made my share of good-natured jokes about Sealy. But, in retrospect, I feel fortunate that I was raised there. It's true that I was nowhere near as worldly as most kids from the city were. But unlike some city kids, I also wasn't thrown to the wolves—into pressures and situations I wasn't prepared to handle. I may have grown up slowly, but I had lots of time to see where I was going.

2
GROWING PAINS

Sealy, as I was saying, wasn't exactly Manhattan when it came to recreational opportunities. You could only cruise the main drag a few thousand times before the thrill wore off. Then again, maybe that was good for me. I had plenty of time to play football.

When I was small we played football all the time, out in a field next to our church. First we'd decide on captains, who would then choose players, and then the captains would give out positions. The big shots would get to play quarterback or halfback. Befitting my stature in the neighborhood, I started out as a lineman.

At Sealy Junior High, in seventh and eighth grade, I first became a running back. I'll never forget our first game. I was absolutely terrified, really just running for my life, but I guess my fear was a pretty good motivator. I wound up scoring four touchdowns that day. I liked that. Suddenly people were looking at me differently. Their eyes showed respect.

Back in those days, my ace in the hole was my speed. Even before my skills as an athlete began to blossom, I was always the fastest kid in the neighborhood. In my entire life, I don't recall ever losing a race. When I was in junior high school, I could already beat anyone in high school. When I became a senior in high school, I ran a 9.4 100-yard dash to win the state championship. I've always been able to move.

Even in junior high, though, my coaches thought I had something else that set me apart. They always used to say I had "good eyes." I know—I wore glasses. But that's not what they meant. They were talking about my vision on a football field, my ability to perceive and react to what the defense was doing. It was almost like a sixth sense—instinctively, I could *feel* where the right place to run was. I bring this up for a reason. Whenever people evaluate my success as a runner, they dwell on my speed and size. And that has a lot to do with it. But I think my vision does, too. I can see things that other runners might not.

I also played baseball in junior high school. I was a centerfielder, with good range on defense and a better-than-average bat. For a while, when I'd be fantasizing about my future, I'd dream about playing football *or* baseball. But I quit playing baseball when I got to high school. There just wasn't enough going on. I'd be standing in center field, waiting for a fly ball to come my way, and I'd be practically asleep on my feet.

Football was different: faster, rougher, more intense. And as I continued to excel at it, it did a lot for my self-esteem. I was accomplishing things, and people were taking notice. I wasn't so introverted anymore, and the girls I used to freeze up around didn't seem quite so intimidating. Even better for my health, the guys who used to pick on me were now steering clear. I liked what the game was doing for me and I couldn't wait to play in high school.

Little did I know what was coming.

I entered Sealy High School full of hope, and my freshman season did start well for me. I was playing on the junior varsity team when, midway through the season, I got the news I was hoping for: along with several other JV players, I was promoted

At Sealy High, I also excelled in track. Here I've just won the 200-meter dash at the state track meet.

to the varsity. Fifteen years old and already in the big time.

The coach of the varsity was a man named Ralph Harris. First let me say that today I've got absolutely nothing against Ralph. After I graduated, Ralph admitted that he had had a lot to learn when he was our coach, that there were times when he was out of line. A lot of coaches, even if they could admit their faults to themselves, wouldn't have the nerve to admit them to the public. I respect Ralph for that.

I have to admit, though, that in my first three years of playing for him, I could not stand the man. Ralph gave new meaning to the term *hardass*.

As I immediately found out, Ralph was clearly committed to winning. But that might have been the only thing we had in common. I hated, and still hate, to lose football games, too. Actually, I hate to be second in anything, even if it's just playing cards on the Rams' team plane. I just don't like to lose. Sure, I love the *competition* of professional football, to test myself against the best. But mostly I like to win.

I hated losing back in high school, too. But even if I didn't care for it, I also knew losing wasn't the end of my world. Especially not at the high school level, where you're also supposed to be having some fun. But to Ralph, losing was nothing less than disgraceful. His temper tantrums were ugly. He'd kick around chairs and tear things up. One time he tore down a bulletin board. What I hated the most, though, was Ralph always calling us a bunch of losers. I could not stand that.

Our team had both black players and white players, but it seemed to me that most of Ralph's problems were with the blacks. Before he came to Sealy High, Ralph, who is white, had always coached in West Texas. And he had always coached white players. After he left Sealy to coach at the University of Texas, Ralph admitted that coaching his first black athletes, at Sealy, had been a difficult adjustment for him. It definitely showed.

But white, black, or green, when you played for Ralph Harris you lived in a world of rules. Ralph was a strict disciplinarian, a staunch believer in the "team concept." Individuality was for other teams' players. Ralph even regulated the way we could look: your hair could not touch your ears. You could not wear a chain around your neck. For the blacks, there were no big Afros and you couldn't wear your hair in a cornrow. This was 1975. We were young and we wanted to look hip like everyone else. Ralph wouldn't let us and we resented it. When you're in high school those kind of things mean a lot to you.

---

*It was almost like a sixth sense—instinctively, I could **feel** where the right place to run was. Whenever people evaluate my success as a runner, they dwell on my speed and size. That has a lot to do with it. But I think my vision does, too. I can see things that other runners might not.*

The battle lines were already drawn, and drawn clearly, my freshman year. One day Ralph was arguing with one of my friends, a big kid named Henry. They both got hot and Ralph began to provoke him.

"Why don't you hit me?" Ralph was saying. "Why don't you take a shot?"

Henry was big and strong but he never moved. Meanwhile, I was getting all worked up, practically jumping up and down.

I was saying *"Hit him, Henry, hit him!"*

Henry played it smart and never took a swing, and eventually they both cooled out. But for Ralph and me, it was only the beginning.

Late in my freshman year we lost a conference game, 19–7. Win, lose, or tie, Ralph always ran us hard. But after that game he went haywire. The next day he inspected our lockers, looking for any little reason to nail us. If a guy had a sock lying at the bottom of his locker, he was made to run laps. If his shoes were looking messy, laps for that, too. That wasn't so bad in itself. But then Ralph started up with all that loser stuff again. We were sick and tired of hearing it.

Sealy High Tigers. That's me, number 19 in the top row. I almost took O. J. Simpson's number—32—but opted for 19 because I wanted to be independent.

After that game, almost every black player on our team upped and quit. I believe one black player remained on the team. I was one of the players who quit. A part of me was heartbroken, because football meant so much to me. But playing for Ralph wasn't my idea of what high school football was supposed to be all about.

In the summer before our sophmore year, Ralph asked several of the black players back to the team. He came to my house, we talked, and I told him I'd like to think things over. I spoke to Gary Hill, but he was as confused as I was. So I asked my mom. Now, my mom didn't like me playing football to begin with. Every time I got buried under a pile, she got all nervous. But she gave me an honest answer: she told me that I wasn't playing for Ralph Harris, I was playing for myself. That's all she said, but I got her point. I decided to go back.

I think every professional athlete recalls a time when his or her skills suddenly exploded. You're good, then you're real good, then—POW!—suddenly you're dominating.

Time out for a minute. Before I go on, I hope I haven't given you the impression that my friends and I were perfect angels in all of this—because we weren't. When you're young and headstrong and trying to be as cool as all your friends, there are times when you think you know it all. And there were times when we purposely did little things to irk Ralph, to see if he could take it as well as he dished it out. What I'm saying is, we definitely weren't blameless.

When my sophomore year began it appeared that things might have improved. But the honeymoon didn't last. Ralph was still all over us, and we were still defiant. One thing that used to drive Ralph crazy was the black players all running in the back of the group together during laps. He would insist that we were prejudiced against white people. If we weren't, he would say, then why did we all run together? Now that was ridiculous. We ran together because we knew Ralph didn't like it, not because we didn't like the white guys.

I've never been prejudiced toward anyone in my life, and that's one of the nicest things I got from living in Sealy. In a lot of small towns, especially in Texas, the blacks and the whites keep their distance. Sealy was never like that, especially among the kids. True, when I was in first and second grade, I did go to an all-black school. But from third grade on, we were all thrown in together. I grew up together with white kids. I played with them and I argued with them, just as I did with black kids. I hung out at their houses, knew their brothers and their sisters. It all seemed perfectly natural—I never gave it a second thought. When I got to high school, my white teammates were the same people I grew up with. And they were still my friends.

I think every professional athlete recalls a time when his or her skills suddenly exploded. You're good, then you're real good, then—*POW!*—suddenly you're dominating. It happened to me in my junior year. As a freshman and sophomore I'd been platooned between halfback and flanker. But now, for the first time since junior high, I was back playing halfback full-time. I wound up gaining just over 2,000 yards. It was an important year for me—the first time I fully realized how good I was at football, and the first time I seriously began to consider football as a possible career.

Now you know how things turned out. But my junior year at Sealy started out looking like a nightmare.

The trouble started when I showed up late for a football game. It was my fault. We normally showed up for an 8:00 P.M. game at 6:30. The day before the game Ralph had said to get to the park a half hour earlier for this one. But I didn't hear him and I arrived at the park at our normal time. When I arrived late Ralph went off, screaming at me in front of everyone. I had made an honest mistake, and I decided I wasn't going to stand for it. Ralph said the whole team depended on me. I said that was wrong, that the players should depend on themselves. Ralph said I wasn't going to start. I said, shoot, I don't want to start. I said I would go sit in the stands. Ralph told me not to. I stood on the sidelines for almost the entire first half before Ralph put me in. That was the last confrontation we had during the football season, but there was another just around the corner.

After football ended I was playing on Sealy's basketball team, as I had the season before. We were playing against Columbus High. They were rivals and the game turned from being physical to downright ugly. I wound up getting in a fight. Ralph, who was also Sealy's athletic director, immediately kicked me off the basketball team. He also suspended me from playing in any other sports. That included track, which I planned on running that spring, as well as football my senior year. I was livid. I even considered transferring from Sealy High.

While I was weighing my options, Ralph changed his mind. He said I could run track that spring, and play football in the fall, but only under one condition: first I'd have to attend what he called his "sunrise services."

Sunrise services? I definitely didn't like the sound of *that*, but I also didn't have much of a choice. College was only two years off and I needed to get that scholarship. This was no time to play the martyr.

I told Ralph I'd do what he said. He told me to be at school on Monday at 6:30 in the morning—dressed for exercise. So that was what sunrise services meant. Wonderful.

I started with a 440-meter dash. Then a 330. Then a 220. Then several 100s. Then I had to run the steps of the stadium. This went on for two weeks, with Ralph eyeballing my every move. I have to admit there were times when I wanted to quit, but I wasn't going to let him break me. I had too much at stake.

IT ISN'T SEALY, BUT I LIKE IT

I really enjoy living in Los Angeles. There's a lot to like: the scenery, the excitement, the climate. I also like the attitude—you can do your own thing, you don't always have to conform.

At first, though, it blew my mind. What amazed me the most was the way people dressed. In L.A. you can wear something absolutely mind-boggling and no one bats an eye. Because, chances are, there's a guy within 15 feet of you who's wearing something even weirder.

Sealy, of course, was a whole different story. If someone in Sealy dressed the way people in L.A. do, someone would call the cops to take them away. You should see my mom when she comes to visit: she's in a constant state of disbelief. We were at the South Coast Mall one day and there was a guy wearing a paper bag as a shirt. No kidding. My mom just couldn't understand it, and she kept asking what was wrong with the guy. I told her that's just how people dress out here—they'll wear anything. Then she looked at me like *I* was nuts.

Another time we saw a punk rocker with his hair all spiked up—I'm talking long, thin, greased-up spikes, pointing straight up to the sky. The kind you can roast marshmallows on. My mom didn't say a word. She just stood there with her eyes as big as quarters.

Maybe he was sick of the aggravation. Maybe he saw the error of his ways. Maybe he knew how good our football team was, and he just didn't want to blow his shot at coaching a big winner. For whatever reasons, Ralph cooled out during my senior year of football. Ralph apologized to me personally; he admitted that he'd been doing some things wrong. I told him that I'd been wrong, too. And I meant it. For a while there I had forgotten what my mother had always told me about humility. People kept telling me how great I was, and at times I began to believe them.

But that all changed my senior year, and Ralph and I didn't have a single problem. As I said, today I've got no hard feelings toward Ralph. Although I never would have admitted it then, he made me a better football player.

My senior year was a dream season. I gained 2,642 yards, with 37 touchdowns. I definitely wasn't a one-man team though. Our team was stacked with speed and talent and we blew people away. We went into our final game with a record of 14-0. It was against Wylie High, a school from just outside of Dallas. The winner would be the Class AA state champions.

The town of Sealy went nuts. The title game was played in Waco, about 140 miles away. And if anyone wanted to rob Sealy that night, he could have walked right in and cleaned it out. Sealy looked like a ghost town—all of its people were out in Waco. Something like 13 buses were chartered to Waco, and the rest of Sealy was jammed into its cars. My grandmother, driving to the game from Houston, stopped off in Sealy to get some gas. She couldn't even find an open gas station and she had to drive on to another town. There was a joke going around Sealy the day of the game: "Last one out of Sealy shut off the lights."

Wylie's lights got turned out, too. We crushed them, 42-20. I scored four touchdowns and ran for 296 yards. Not a bad way to end things: Sealy High, Class AA state champs.

Later that night, back in Sealy, the 7-Eleven was hopping.

3
COLLEGE KID

When I graduated from Sealy High School, I was barely 18 years old. And, already, the heat was on.

I had gained nearly 6,000 yards in three high school seasons. As a senior I was a *Parade* All-American and some people were calling me the best high school running back in the nation. Suddenly I was getting all kinds of attention. Celebrated college coaches, coaches who I'd seen on TV, were flying across the country to sell me on their schools. Reporters from prestigious papers wanted to know about the place where I grew up.

My head was spinning, but at first I loved every minute of it. For a small-town boy—shoot, for anyone—it was intoxicating.

Then the scouts moved in.

They had started trickling to our games when I was a junior. By my senior year it had turned into a tidal wave. There must have been 10 or 12 scouts at every game. When it came to the crunch time—when I was making my final decision—Sealy looked like a national scout convention. These guys were all over town, but mostly they came to my house. There'd be a few with my mom in the kitchen, another sitting in his car in front of our house, and another down the block waiting to make his move. I was afraid a couple of scouts might move in next door: *BOOM!*—there goes the neighborhood.

Seriously, though, some of these guys had no shame. I couldn't believe the things I was hearing. They'd call me on the phone and they'd literally be begging me to go to their school. Some guys sounded on the verge of tears. "Please," they'd sob, "I'll lose my job if we don't get you." It was mind-boggling: I was a senior in high school and grown men were begging me to play football for them.

They were driving my mother crazy. My mom developed high blood pressure about that time, and she still insists it's from my recruitment. There isn't any question that some college scouts couldn't care less who they hurt. They'd call and wake up the house late at night, or come knocking on the door at six in the morning. For a while I was tempted to hide out at my friends' houses. But then they would have ganged up on my mom.

Then the scouts moved in. There'd be a few with my mom in the kitchen, another sitting in his car in front of our house, and another down the block waiting to make his move. I was afraid a couple of scouts might move in next door: BOOM!—there goes the neighborhood.

Did the scouts bad-mouth other schools? Does Elizabeth Taylor like to get wedding gifts? They'd tell me: "You want to go *there*? That's the *last* place you want to go to. Do you know what they *do* over there?" Two minutes after telling me how sleazy the school down the road was, they'd offer me the moon, the stars, and maybe Halley's Comet just for good measure. They'd tell me that they would do this or that for my family, that my mother would never have to work again. Some guys would offer me

Ron Meyer and Steve Endicott were two of my coaches at SMU. Ron later coached the New England Patriots.

Here I'm a senior in high school; the next year I was recruited by colleges across the country.

money just to come visit their campuses. The entire courtship was beginning to sicken me. It's a cliché, but I felt like a piece of meat.

Some guys sounded on the verge of tears. "Please," they'd sob, "I'll lose my job if we don't get you." Some college scouts couldn't care less who they hurt. They'd call and wake up the house late at night, or come knocking on the door at six in the morning.

That's the down side. On the other hand, some of the scouts and coaches I met were perfect gentlemen. My senior year, John Robinson flew out to see me from the University of Southern California. I was excited—I had watched John's teams on TV and I always figured I'd like him. In person he didn't let me down. John had an easy smile and there wasn't any hard sell. He wasn't crying and slobbering like some of the other coaches and scouts.

"I really like USC," I told him, "but it's a little too far away for me. I'm going to go to Oklahoma."

"Well, good luck," John said. "I'm sorry we can't get you. You're a good one."

And that was that.

You see, at that point my heart was set on Oklahoma. I liked everything about the Sooners. They had a lot of Texas boys. They were always on TV, always going to bowls, and they seemed so glamorous. With their wishbone offense, they were obviously committed to their running game. I also liked their coach, Barry Switzer. Barry came to Waco to watch our state championship game and he also visited my house twice. Barry seemed friendly and loose, someone who wouldn't be hung up on silly rules. Someone you could win with, but someone who would also be fun to play for.

My mom felt differently.

> ## WHY I WEAR A LOT OF PADS
>
> I wear a lot of pads for a good reason: I want to play football, not sit on the sideline with an injury. Wearing a lot of pads isn't something that started when I got to the NFL. I've worn a lot of pads ever since high school. My philosophy is basically this: if they make it, and it will save my body, then I'll wear it. People think my pads slow me down, but they don't in any way because they're designed to be light. If they slowed me down I wouldn't wear them.

In fact, my mom didn't like anything about Barry. She thought he was sneaky. Most of all, she thought he talked too much about Billy Sims, who was then the big gun at OU.

"All that man ever talks about is Billy Sims," she kept saying. "Why you want to go down there with Billy Sims?"

I was torn, to say the least. I'd make up my mind—once and for all, absolutely for sure—then I'd change it. My mom was dead set against Oklahoma, and not just because of Barry. She said she wanted me to stay in Texas so she could come see me play. She urged me to go to Southern Methodist University, which was in Dallas, only 200 miles from Sealy. She was also taken by the SMU coach, who was then Ron Meyer. (Ron was smart—he talked about my education and immediately got my mom on his side.) I liked Ron, too. He seemed sincere and he was one of the few coaches who never ripped another school. When I told him I was impressed by Oklahoma, he just said, "Well, that's a fine institution."

It was a stalemate: my mom for SMU, me for Oklahoma. Finally, reluctantly, I agreed to go to SMU. My heart wasn't really in it though. I did it for one reason only: out of respect for my mother.

The problem was, it wasn't my mom who had to go there.

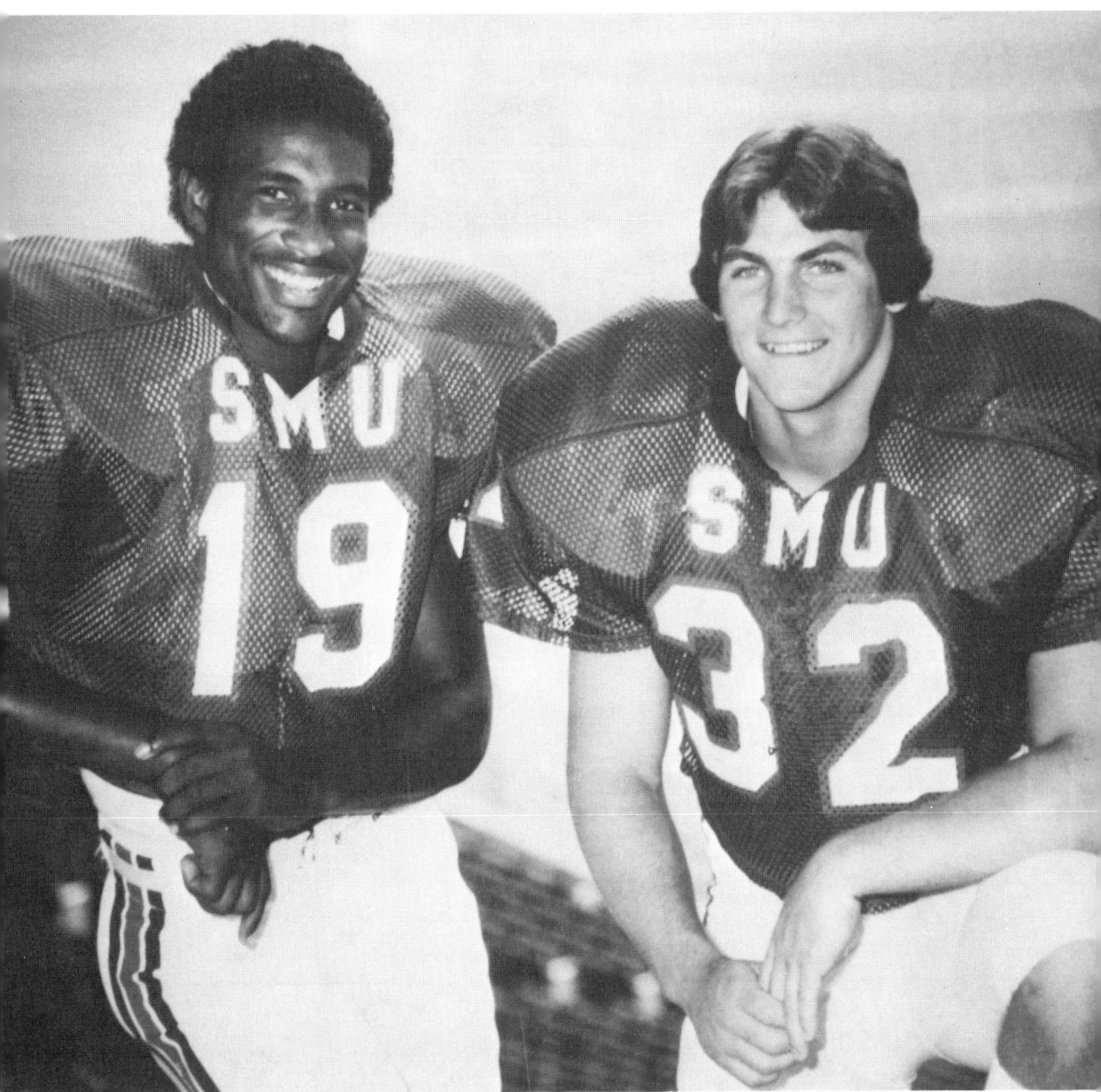

At SMU, Craig James and I teamed up for what the press called "the Pony Express." Neither of us cared for it at first, but we eventually grew to accept it.

College Kid

When *I* got there I hated it. I hated the school and I hated Dallas. I felt I had been cheated, like I never should have gone there in the first place. Every Sunday I went back to Sealy. When it was time to return to Dallas, they practically had to stuff me into my car.

Part of it was simple, just freshman homesick blues; I'd never lived on my own before. But getting culture shock from living in a big city like Dallas really wasn't a problem—because the summer before my senior year I had spent a lot of time in Houston, which is much bigger than Dallas, and I had fallen in love with it. I think my hate for Dallas was more a matter of not *wanting* to like it. I was fighting it every step of the way.

It was a stalemate: my mom for SMU, me for Oklahoma. Finally, reluctantly, I agreed to go to SMU. I did it for one reason only: out of respect for my mother. When I got there I hated it. I hated the school and I hated Dallas.

My situation with women didn't help. I couldn't believe it—SMU didn't have any black women. It seemed like 99.9 percent of the women on campus were white. The only way to meet black women was to go off campus. As unhappy and uneasy as I was, I rarely felt adventurous enough to check out the city of Dallas. So I just didn't date much.

Things weren't much better on the playing field. Everyone likes to get greeted by new teammates with open arms. All I got was cold shoulders.

Later I found out why. I'd come to SMU surrounded by hype, and some of my teammates didn't care for it. Then, when I got there, the coaches just handed me the starting tailback position. I didn't even have to work for it. Here was this high school phenom who was going to start at tailback. That especially didn't sit well with the other backs. So they would purposely freeze me

At first I didn't even want to be at SMU—I didn't like anything about it. By the time graduation came I didn't want to leave.

from their conversations. The backs would all be sitting in a circle prior to practice, talking and getting stretched, and I'd come and ask them what they were talking about.

"Nothing *you'd* know about." "Why are you so *nosy*?"

One freshman, Charles Drayton, was particularly hard on me. He was a freshman tailback who had redshirted the year before. At first Charles wouldn't even acknowledge my existence. But we wound up as suitemates in the freshman dorm, and I guess Charles ran out of ways to avoid me. Once the initial barrier was broken, we took to each other immediately. Charles grew up in Indiantown, Florida, population 2,000, and we found we had a lot in common. Once we got tight, I asked Charles why he'd been so cool. He said he had gotten sick of reading in the newspaper about this so-called savior from Sealy. With all the press he was sure I had to be an egomaniac.

Charles and I roomed together for two years at SMU. Later, when I moved west to play for the Rams, Charles found work there, too, and for about 18 months we shared an apartment. I live alone now, but Charles is still my closest friend. He's like the brother I always wanted but never had.

As my season progressed I was fully accepted by my teammates, but I was still struggling on the field. Nagged by injuries, I carried the ball just 115 times for 477 yards. Worse, the team was only 5–5. Meanwhile, Oklahoma was on its way to the Orange Bowl. That really burned me. I could have been a part of that—but, no. I had to go to SMU.

I returned to SMU for my sophomore year. But after I found out how the coaches were planning on using me, I wondered why I did. That was the year I became one-half of what the media called "the Pony Express." Coach Meyer had Craig James and me alternating at tailback on every offensive possession. If we had a 15-play drive, I'd play for 15 plays. If we had three plays and a punt, I'd play for just those three plays. I hated it. I had never played in a system like that and I didn't want to now.

Mostly I was frustrated by my lack of carries. I'm a big back

> ## *I LIKE YOU TOO, BUT LET'S NOT GET CARRIED AWAY*
>
> I like to be kissed—as long as it's by a woman. The craziest encounter I ever had with a fan was in the parking lot following a home game. While signing some autographs near my car, I was approached by a middle-aged man. I didn't know what he wanted, and if I had, I would have run the other way. This guy reached out, grabbed me, and started kissing me on the neck. No kidding—he had both of my arms locked down and he was kissing me. "I love you," he was saying. "I really, really love you." It's nice to be appreciated, but come on.

and I feel I can wear people down as a game goes on. And carrying the ball a lot is just like doing anything else a lot: you slide into a groove, where it all seems almost automatic. Now I was coming out on every other possession, screwing up my groove. But most of all, I just never saw myself as a part-time player.

Craig and I, both prideful people, didn't like the Pony Express at all. People have asked me if it put any strains on our relationship. Not in the least—we never had a single harsh word. Craig's a good guy. I was pleased at his success in the 1985 season with New England.

As for the SMU coaches, well, I wasn't real pleased with them. It may have been purely coincidence, but it seemed like Craig was getting more playing time than I was. I wound up with 928 yards, a decent season, but I felt I could have contributed so much more. After all, my average yards per carry was 7.9. I couldn't help myself: I wanted to be out there on every play. And I still wasn't feeling good about SMU.

To make matters worse, I also didn't care for some of the stories people were writing about me in the press. For reasons I still don't comprehend, they were questioning my heart. A couple of writers suggested that Craig should be the only tailback. What was going on? Here I was busting my butt and still I was getting ripped. Maybe I was overly sensitive, still fighting the world because I didn't really want to be there. But I felt unwanted and unappreciated, as if everyone at SMU was against me. It was not a good time in my life.

Back in Oklahoma, word got out that I'd called coach Barry Switzer to transfer and he hadn't been in his office to take the call. One of the local headlines cracked me up: "BARRY, WHERE WERE YOU WHEN ERIC CALLED?"

That spring I decided to transfer. One day I picked up the phone and called Barry Switzer. This time I was serious—I was going to ask him about coming to Oklahoma. When Barry's secretary got on the line, she said that Barry was not in his office. She asked if I wanted to leave my name and number. Don't ask me why, but I told her no. I said I would just call back.

I never made that call. Because soon after I tried to call Barry, my mom moved into the picture. When I told her I wanted to transfer to Oklahoma she was upset. She said I hadn't given SMU enough of a chance, and she couldn't understand my obsession with Oklahoma.

"If you go to Oklahoma," my mom wanted to know, "are you guaranteed to start?"

"No."

"Is it guaranteed you won't get hurt?"

"No."

"Then what the heck is guaranteed there?"

"... Nothing."

"Then why don't you just stay where you're at?"

Put to me like that, I didn't have a very good answer. Maybe my mom was right, maybe I hadn't given SMU enough of a chance. I decided not to transfer.

(Meanwhile, back in Oklahoma, word got out that I'd called Barry to transfer and he hadn't been in his office to take the call. One of the local headlines cracked me up: "BARRY, WHERE WERE YOU WHEN ERIC CALLED?")

Sometimes I still wonder: If Barry had been in his office, how would my life have been different? As it was, my mom was right again: I wound up absolutely loving SMU. I loved it so much that, when graduation rolled around, I couldn't even stand the thought of leaving. That taught me two valuable lessons:

- Don't be so impatient: give things a chance to develop.
- My mom has excellent advice.

I almost hate to admit it, but as a junior and senior I even grew to accept the Pony Express. It was kind of funny—by the time we were seniors, it was Craig who was complaining that *he* didn't get the ball enough. Looking back, I think the Pony Express might even have prolonged my career in the pros. You see a lot of young runners come out of college with knee problems. When I got to the NFL my legs were fresh.

My career at SMU mirrored my development in high school: I came into my own my last two seasons. As a junior I gained 1,428 yards, with an average of 5.6 yards per carry and 19 touchdowns. Senior year I had 1,617 yards, an average of 7.0 and 17 TDs. As a senior I had runs of 80, 80, 79, 70, 63, and 62 yards. Both seasons I was voted Offensive Player of the Year in the Southwest Conference. For my career I had 4,450 yards, an average of 5.6, 47 touchdowns, and 27 100-yard-plus games. Both years I was All-American, and as a senior I was third behind Herschel Walker and John Elway in the Heisman Trophy balloting.

As for SMU, we were 10–1 when I was a junior and 10–0–1 my last year. And my senior year we finally got to go to our bowl game, beating Dan Marino and Pittsburgh in the Cotton Bowl.

I was on the run again, this time for the pros.

4
WELCOME TO THE PROS

The thing that drove me nuts was the wondering.

It was a Friday in April 1983, and the NFL draft was just a few days off. It's an odd sensation waiting for the draft. Nothing less than your future is on the line, yet it's basically in other people's hands. You could wind up on a longtime loser or on a team that's on its way to the Super Bowl. In Indianapolis or in New York. Sure, you could make an educated guess depending on who is picking when, but even then a last-moment trade can change everything. And when it comes to the draft, it's not like you have a whole lot of leverage. Unless you want to play in Canada, or the United States Football League, or nowhere at all, then you go where you're drafted.

My own first choice was the Los Angeles Rams.

True, I hadn't been a Rams fan all my life. When I was in high school my favorite team was the Pittsburgh Steelers. Back in those days they were dominating the league, but I liked the Steelers for another reason: they wore the same colors—black and gold—that Sealy High did.

In college I started liking the Rams, and I also decided that they were the team I wanted to play for. I had liked John Robinson ever since I met him in high school. Like Texas, the weather in California was warm, good weather for running with a football. Most important, the Rams had a history of winning. In high school and then in college I'd gotten used to winning. It was a habit I liked.

Since 1972 the Rams have failed to make the playoffs just twice. The first time was 1981, the second was 1982, the year that I was a senior at SMU. Playing in the strike-shortened season, in Ray Malavasi's final year as coach, they were only 2–7. Normally I rooted for the Rams to win, but that year I was pulling for them to lose. I knew if they kept losing they'd have a shot at drafting me.

"Go with the NFL," said my mom. "They've been around a lot longer than that other league. At least you know they'll be there."

The Rams wound up with the third pick in the draft. I knew that they were clearly interested in me, but I also saw that I was in danger of already being picked by the time they drafted. The Colts drafted first and seemed certain to nab John Elway. (Later he was traded to Denver.) But the Oilers, choosing second, still hadn't tipped their hand as the draft approached.

Now, the Friday before Tuesday's draft, I was sitting at home when the phone rang. I couldn't believe it—it was John Robinson, who was entering his first season as coach of the Rams. John said the Rams definitely wanted to get me, but he was worried about the Oilers. He said he was going to try to work something out with them. I thanked him, hung up, and began to hold my breath. I was dying to play for the Rams.

On Monday I heard the news: the Rams and Oilers had

Running comes naturally to me. I've always gotten a kick out of it, whether it's on a football field or out near my home.

I can think of more enjoyable things to do in my spare time than lifting weights. But in the NFL it's a fact of life.

Welcome to the Pros

exchanged places in the draft, with the Oilers receiving a pair of draft choices. I was running around the house going wild. On Tuesday I was drafted by the Rams!

Complications arose that summer. As they often do, they came in the form of money. Looking toward its second season, the USFL was again battling the NFL for the top graduating seniors. The owners of the new league were throwing around some serious dollars, and I was one of the people they really wanted.

In July the Los Angeles Express made me their offer. It was extremely substantial, considerably more than the Rams' best offer. I told the Express I'd like to think things over. Again I was faced with a choice. On the one hand my heart was set on playing for the Rams, in the NFL. But when someone else offers you that kind of money, and shows you that kind of interest, you've at least got to give it some thought.

I called my mom to see what she thought. She told me she wanted to sleep on it, to call her back in the morning.

I called her in the morning.

"Go with the NFL," she said. "They've been around a lot longer than that other league. At least you know they'll be there."

Coming from my mom, that was all I needed to hear. I had been leaning heavily toward the Rams regardless. That night I signed with the Rams.

John Robinson pumps people up better than any coach I've ever played for. It doesn't matter if you're the team's best player or the third-string punter, John will have you believing you're a lock for the Hall of Fame.

My first day on the job was unusual. It was a preseason minicamp and we were practicing some running plays. I thought everything was going fine, but Coach Robinson apparently didn't. Every time I carried the ball, he kept on yelling to me.

"You got to go *faster*, Eric! You got to *explode* through that hole! You got to hit it *faster!*"

I was confused. I was running the same way I had in college and in high school, the same way I'd been running ever since I started playing football. But John just kept on yelling. Finally I spoke up.

"Coach Robinson, I *am* running as fast as I can.

"I'll tell you what," I went on, "Let's run across this field together. Then you'll see how fast I'm running."

John started laughing.

Later on, I found out why John thought I wasn't running my hardest: because I didn't *look* to him like I was. Although John had seen my game films dozens of times, films are never the same as watching someone in person. So on that first day of practice, John thought he was getting a typical "big, fast back." Most backs like that, John said, aren't real fluid when they run. They also make a lot of noise as they bull down the field. John figured I'd be the same way. But John was surprised when he saw me himself, surprised at how smoothly I ran. He said I barely made any noise at all.

My teammates planted me with another nickname. They started calling me "Mr. Benny." That's after the late Jack Benny. As in cheap.

Then again, John is always saying nice things about his players—it's one of the reasons they remain so loyal. Ever since that first day of practice, my own relationship with John has been excellent. Every successful coach has his own particular strength, and I think John's is motivating his players. And that is a direct result of his personality. It doesn't matter at what level you're playing, the last thing you want is some deadhead coach who's got no charisma. Coaches like that can lull a team to sleep.

WILL SOMEONE PLEASE TURN ON THE LIGHTS?

Someone recently asked me if I could recall the hardest hit I ever took. That's a difficult question for a player in the NFL—I get mashed like a potato every game. Really getting drilled is a feeling that's hard to describe. I've been hit so hard it was as if my body just went into shock. As if I'd been struck by a high-voltage wire. There have been times when my body went all numb, times when I got up and my eyes were crossed. But no matter how hard I'm hit, I never let on that I'm hurt. I never want the other team to know when I'm hurt.

One hit when I was a rookie does stand out in my mind. It was against the Buffalo Bills and I don't even remember the name of the guy who hit me. I think he was a defensive end or a linebacker. It was a pitch-out and the defense called a blitz. The split second I got the ball—*CRASH!*—he struck me in the face with his helmet. The first thing that hit the ground was the back of my head. I stumbled to my feet but felt like I was about to black out. Everything starting going dark, then I saw a bunch of little white dots in front of my face. I started counting—one, two, three, four, five—thinking, "Don't black out, don't black out." When I got back to the huddle, I told the guys I thought I was going to black out. They said, "OK, we won't call your number this play." That was the hardest I've ever been hit, and I don't even know the guy's name.

You want a guy who's *alive*, who pumps people up. John pumps people up better than any coach I've ever played for. It doesn't matter if you're the team's best player or the third-string punter, John will have you believing you're a lock for the Hall of Fame. That's important, because football players have doubts and fears just like anyone else. John makes you feel invincible.

Personally, I also prefer playing for a coach who I feel comfortable talking with. I can talk to John as I can one of my friends. John has a temper and he doesn't hesitate to tell people when he's upset, but he also doesn't get off on playing dictator. He loves to win football games, but he also likes to enjoy the ride. John likes to keep things loose. Sometimes we'll finish a meeting and everyone will jump up to leave, but John won't let us go until someone tells a new joke. Those are little things, but they're the kinds of little things that make a team close. John has the common touch; he likes people and people like him.

The Rams also hold a Mr. Ugly Contest. When your team is as ugly as ours is, you have to break it down into categories. There are awards for the Ugliest Black Guy, Ugliest White Guy, Ugliest Guy Over 30, Ugliest Guy in the Front Office, Ugliest Coach, etc. For the biggest ugly of them all, there's Grand Champion Ugly.

As for my first encounter with my teammates, I wasn't sure what to expect. As a freshman at SMU, my teammates had decided not to like me before they even got to know me. I was hoping it would be different in the pros, but who could tell? Maybe they'd resent me for my contract. Although it certainly wasn't anything special compared to the contracts of other first-round picks, I would still be making more money as a rookie than some guys who'd been playing for several years. In pro sports, it's a fact of life that rookies often get more money than the veterans. It's part of today's game. But that doesn't mean the veterans like it.

I decided just to be myself. Either they would accept me or they wouldn't. And it worked—I never felt a hint of coldness or resentment. Don't get me wrong—it's not like I was one of the boys overnight. It was a gradual process. But it did happen, while

Welcome to the Pros

for some rookies it never does—they come in cocky or moody and they never get accepted. I could never play football like that. Being close to my teammates means a lot to me. Football can wear you down. Having buddies makes it much more fun.

That's not to say that I didn't have to pay my dues. First-round pick or last-round pick, I was still a rookie. Meaning that I still had to take my share of kidding. My teammates started calling me "Number One," as in number-one draft choice. It was "Hey, Number One, grab that football." Or "Hey, Number One, why don't you go talk to that girl?" One time at dinner they made me sing "Old McDonald Had a Farm." When I got through butchering that, they thought I might be on safer ground with my college

I'm 6'3" and 220 pounds today. But when I was a kid, I was tall and skinny. I began to fill out in college.

HARD BUT CLEAN

Cheap shots are not very prevalent in the NFL. Most of the guys prefer to play hard but clean. It's interesting that when people talk about cheap-shotting players, they're almost always talking about defensive players. People don't realize that offensive players, if they wanted to, could play dirty, too. Even a running back. One way would be to wait until a defensive player is tangled with a blocker, then cut out his legs from the side. I've seen it happen, but I would never, ever do that. I'm not going to endanger a man's career just so I can take revenge.

If someone is playing dirty against me, and I want to send him a message, I like to stay within the rules. So my favorite weapon is the stiff-arm. Walter Payton and Marcus Allen, among other running backs, throw good ones too. Stiff-arming doesn't work well against the size and bulk of the defensive linemen, but it seems to do the job with the defensive backs, who are often my size or smaller. What I do is wait until the final moment. When a defensive back is coming at me with his hands out and his head down, I'll wait and then I'll just *stiff* him, right in his face. I've caught some guys by surprise and knocked their helmets right off. Not only does it embarrass the heck out of them, but, man, does it get them hot. One guy told me he was going to break my hand.

fight song. They were wrong. I had no idea how it went, so I tried to fake it by making up the words. That didn't work either. Finally the guys began to lose their appetites, and I was mercifully allowed to stop.

Being wise guys, when they got tired of Number One, my teammates planted me with another nickname. They started calling me "Mr. Benny." That's after the late Jack Benny. As in cheap.

Welcome to the Pros

Why am I posing next to a weight machine? Good question. Actually I'm doing a layout for a fitness magazine.

56   **ON THE RUN**

If you've never been tackled by Lawrence Taylor, don't feel too bad about it. Believe me, there are better things you can do with your time.

This is a commercial for the United Way. I like doing things like this. It's my way of helping other people, of saying thanks.

Before my first year with the Rams I told a friend I'd be happy if I gained 1,200 yards. I exceeded my own expectations.

It started my rookie year. Before the season I wanted to stay in Sealy with my family as long as I could, and I arrived in Los Angeles without much time to look for an apartment. I hate looking for places to stay in the first place, and I just grabbed whatever I could find. This turned out to be a modest little apartment, which I promptly made even more modest by barely stocking it with any furniture. I knew I wouldn't be staying there long, so why go and buy a bunch of things that might not fit into

In the middle of a season, there are so many demands, sometimes an athlete doesn't have time to just sit down and think. I value the off-season, in part because I can spend some time alone.

For any young runners out there, this isn't the ideal way to carry the ball. However, in the heat of a game, when a guy is ripping your shoulder off, you do what you can.

another place? To me it made sense. To everyone else I was cheap.

I have to say that I think there are a lot worse qualities a person can have than being mindful of his money. But, as long as we're on the subject, I might as well set the record straight. I do not sit home at night and count my pennies. I don't throw dollar bills around like they're Refrigerator Perrys. I do buy things I like, things I need.

At the same time, I don't take my money and lose my mind with it. Even if I had all the money in the world, there are some things I would still never buy. I live close to the Pacific Ocean and

Practice isn't thrilling, but it gives us a chance to work out the rough spots and try new things. On the Rams we take them seriously.

The Saints are not a perennial power, but they usually play the Rams pretty tough.

people always ask me when I'm going to buy a boat. When I'm on water I feel as if a band is playing inside my stomach. Now, what do I need a boat for?

It goes back to the way I was raised. We didn't have a lot of money and I was taught to appreciate the value of a dollar. My mother taught me to be frugal, and I'm glad she did. When I retire from football, I don't want to be one of those guys you read

THE PRESS AND I

Let me say, for the record, that I have nothing against the press as a whole. There are good athletes and bad ones, and the same goes for the people in the media. L.A. has some fine writers. What gets me mad is when I say one thing and something entirely different gets printed in the paper. It has happened to me several times and it's annoying. Those are the writers I try to steer clear of.

If you follow the Rams, you're probably aware that there are times when I'll get feisty with the guys who are covering the team, when I'll talk right back to them. I can't help it, they just get me so mad sometimes. Running against 11 men who are trying to tear your head off is *hard*. But some reporters seem to forget that.

So one time I told the reporters that if any of them felt they could do a better job than I was doing, they were invited to come and do it, and have my salary too. Of course no one took me up on my offer, and I was kind of disappointed. If a press guy ever did agree to line up in the backfield, I guarantee you that every defensive player in the league would be fighting to line up against him. Even I would like to play a little defense for that.

about going bankrupt. I want to be able to provide for the people who are close to me.

Of course none of this matters to my teammates. They love calling me Mr. Benny and they're not going to stop for some mere technicalities. I'm happy to say, though, that I'm hardly the only Ram who serves as the butt of jokes. My teammates are very big on jokes, any kind of jokes, but they're especially fond of the practical kind. Just ask Jackie Slater.

Jackie ran out to practice one day thinking everything was business as usual. Except it wasn't. Jackie was standing around

That's me and Barry Redden, another running back, catching a breather along the Rams sideline.

when suddenly his eyes got all big. Then he started jumping around like a wild man. Finally he sprinted back to the locker room, looking curiously like a man in severe distress. The rest of us, in the meantime, were all lying on the grass cracking up, because we knew exactly what Jackie's problem was. Before he got dressed for practice, someone had kidnapped Jackie's jock and lined it with balm—not just any balm, but the kind that throws off terrible heat. Bob Seger once wrote a song called "Fire Down Below." Jackie's one guy who can really relate to it.

We also hold a Mr. Ugly Contest. We do it each year and we all take it very seriously. When your team is as ugly as ours is, you have to break it down into categories. So that's what we do. There's awards for the Ugliest Black Guy, Ugliest White Guy, Ugliest Guy Over 30, Ugliest Guy in the Front Office, Ugliest Coach, etc. For the biggest ugly of them all, there's Grand Champion Ugly. Every year we have a big ceremony where the, uh, winners get announced. Last year we did it in Atlanta and we even gave out trophies—little figurines with bags over their heads.

I know: you want to know who won. But I'm not going to tell you. I've gotta play with these guys all season. And you know how touchy ugly people can get.

I was terrified before my first pro scrimmage. Palms-sopping, throat-like-a-desert terrified.

It was a scrimmage against the Dallas Cowboys, whose summer camp was just up the road in Thousand Oaks, California. Our rookies against their rookies, at Cal State Fullerton. It's where we practice, and I should have been comfortable. I should have been, but I wasn't. In fact, I was so jittery my mind went completely blank in the middle of the scrimmage. I couldn't remember a thing—not a play, not a formation, not anything. When I ran off the field I hurried over to our running-back coach, Bruce Snyder.

There's nothing like the feeling of finding a big hole and taking off for the end zone.

"Bruce, I can't remember *anything*. What do I do?"

Bruce told me to just calm down, to pull myself together. Eventually I regained my grip and remembered the plays. But as far as beginnings go, mine won't make any highlights films.

Our first regular-season game was against the New York Giants. The Giants had an outside linebacker named Lawrence Taylor. If you've never been tackled by Lawrence Taylor, don't feel too bad about it. Believe me, there are better things you can do with your time. Going into the game I had heard all about Mr. Taylor and I wasn't real anxious to see if it was true. But everything turned out fine. I had a few collisions with Lawrence, but I was ready for him. We even had a conversation as I walked by him following one play.

"I'm gonna get your ass," he said. "I'm gonna get you."

"Come on, Lawrence," I told him, "you've got to do better than that."

Lawrence just laughed.

I got plenty of work in my first pro game—31 carries for 91 yards. More important, we beat the Giants, 16–6.

Two weeks later, I was the goat.

We were playing against the Green Bay Packers. In the final quarter, with 33 seconds left, the score was tied, 24–24. We had the ball on our 20-yard-line and our plan was to run out the clock, then try and win in overtime. The play was a simple handoff to me. But just as I was about to take the ball, I began to slip. I fumbled the ball, and the Packers recovered. Two plays later they beat us with a field goal.

I felt miserable, as if I was the reason we lost. Deep down I knew I wasn't—no single play can lose a 48-minute game—but I still felt lousy. For one thing, I knew I'd catch hell in L.A. newspapers. I did and I was totally embarrassed. To this day it's still my biggest embarrassment as a pro. But what could I do about it? I had screwed up and nothing could change that. The key was to come back strong the next week.

My first three pro games were decent but hardly spectacular.

I gained 91, 88, and 75 yards. My longest run was 24 yards. After the Green Bay game, what I needed to turn things around was perfectly clear to me: that one long run. A long run can break another team's back, as well as get your own team all fired up. In college, whenever I got a long run, it usually turned out to be contagious. Several more would follow. Going into the fourth game of the season, against the New York Jets, I was still looking for that first one as a pro.

It was early in the opening quarter, our second play from scrimmage. I swept around left end and saw some daylight. I got a few beautiful blocks, outran a couple of defensive backs, and I was gone. Eighty-five yards for a touchdown. I finished the day with 192 yards. It felt just like old times.

I felt bad about the game, which we lost, but I was still excited that I had finally busted loose. It was exactly what our offense needed.

From that point on, my rookie year went better than I'd ever dreamed it could. Before the season began, I talked to Charlie Drayton about what I hoped to accomplish: I told Charlie that if I could gain about 1,200 yards and get about six touchdowns, that would be a great rookie season.

I wasn't trying to limit myself, it's just that I had heard how different, how much tougher, the NFL would be from college. Like night and day, people told me, like nothing I ever experienced. So much bigger, so much faster, so much stronger. I was expecting a league of supermen.

Once I started playing, I knew better.

I'm not saying the pros aren't tougher than college. They are. And the differences are very real. In college the holes close fast, but in the pros they'll close with you right inside them. In the pros you've got 250-pound linebackers who run like fullbacks and 300-pound linemen who run like linebackers. What amazed me most was the skill of the defensive backs. These guys can cover anything. You make a move, they're there. You make another, they're still right in your face. Some of these guys were

Welcome to the Pros

5'9" or 5'10" and they were running right with me. That was a big shock for someone who has a lot of pride in his speed.

However, once I got into the pros, I realized I was just as good as the people I was playing with. They were flesh and blood just like me. They didn't have anything that I didn't.

As I was saying, everything turned around after that Jets game. The next week against the Lions, I had 199 yards. I wound up with nine 100-yard games and a season total of 1,808. I scored 20 touchdowns. I led the league in rushing and was named the NFL Rookie of the Year. Considering the conversation I had had with Charlie, I have to admit it: in my rookie year, I surprised even myself.

As for the Rams, we finished only 9–7, but we made it to the playoffs. After beating Dallas in the opening round, we got blown out by Washington. That was totally humiliating, something I never want to go through again. But we didn't let it tarnish our season. We'd gone from 2–7 to the second round of the playoffs—we felt we had turned things around.

The future would prove us right.

You can't see my linemen in this picture, but you can bet they're the reason I found this hole.

5
CLOSING IN ON O.J.

Across the line of scrimmage, the Houston Oilers were talking trash.

It was December 1984, my second year in the pros, the Rams' 15th game of the regular season. I wasn't exactly a hardened veteran, but there was one thing I'd grown used to: in the course of a game, when tempers are short, language on the field gets pretty nasty.

Sometimes it's just the heat of the moment; it's a physical game played by emotional people. Other times the talking has a purpose—to try to intimidate you, get you looking over your shoulder. Or to try to distract you, get you so enraged that you forget about your assignment. It's never bothered me, and I can't see it bothering most players, but people keep talking.

Sometimes you hear some things out there that are pretty funny. We were playing the New Orleans Saints one day on the road. One of the Saints' best players is Rickey Jackson. Rickey's a linebacker—6'2", 240 pounds—a big hitter who's also got the speed to run you down. He's also one of my friends. After Rickey and I untangled following one play, Rickey tried to snarl at me.

"You aren't getting 100 yards today."

"But, Rickey," I told him, "I've already got 100."

This made Rickey pause for a second.

"Well..." he finally said, "then you aren't getting 200."

Moving from Sealy to California took some adjusting. But I like it a lot here. The climate's great and so is the scenery. And I've wanted to play for the Rams since I was in college.

Closing in on O.J. 73

It's a dream come true—moving faster than the camera can catch me.

There was nothing funny about that game with the Oilers. For us it was a crucial game. We were 9–5, still very much in the race for the playoffs. A win over the Oilers would be a giant step.

The Oilers, on the other hand, were having a season to forget. They were 3–11, their hopes for the playoffs squashed long ago. But there wasn't a man on our team who was taking them lightly.

Here I am, posing for that magazine layout again in the weight room. Meanwhile, out of the picture, my teammates are giving me grief.

Lifting weights is a lot of hard, sweaty work. I think that's obvious from this shot.

No, this is not the Dodgers' Triple A team. It's a celebrity softball team that I play on in Los Angeles. I'll let you pick out the familiar faces.

We knew the Oilers would love nothing better than to take us down with them.

In the week before the game, I found out that something else

was eating at the Oilers. Back in the Houston newspapers, they were building up this game into a personal grudge match. And the object of their fire was me.

I had a pretty good idea why. It had something to do with the time when I was about to be drafted. A local reporter asked me if I had any desire to play for the Oilers. Now, I love the city of Houston, and I love the people, but I still wanted to play for the

Clowning around with some cartoon characters. By the way, I guess you could say I'm a cartoon nut. I guess I've still got some kid in me.

Rams. At the time, the Oilers didn't look as if they were going anywhere.

One of the things I pride myself on is my honesty. There have

been times in my life when I probably should have kept my mouth shut but instead said what was on my mind and wound up getting in trouble. That was one of those times. I told the reporter the truth: no, I didn't want to play for the Oilers.

I should have guessed: the next day it was all over the newspapers and it didn't go over real well with the local sports fans. Texans—like anybody else—tend to take those kinds of things

I still like playing baseball. When I was younger I played center field. But I gave it up for football, which I found to be a lot more exciting.

personally. And the fans weren't alone. Some of the Oilers themselves apparently took it *very* personally. How personally? More than two years later, in the week before their game with us,

they still hadn't forgotten.

It seemed as if my phone never stopped ringing that week. All my buddies back in Texas would call, newspapers right in hand, to read to me the comments from the Oilers. There were a lot of little things said, most of which I just shrugged off. The Oilers were still angry about what I'd said, and I could understand that. But there was one comment that stuck in my throat. The Oilers

I do a lot of charity work and I enjoy it. I especially like working with children. On the occasions when I can provide them with some inspiration, I feel as good as they do.

ME, A FOLDOUT?

If I live to be 200, I don't think I'll ever stop getting kidded by my teammates about the time I posed for *Playgirl* magazine. It was the December 1985 issue. Sandy Friedman, my publicist, thought being in the magazine would be good exposure for me, something different. I agreed to pose, but I made it clear from the start that I wouldn't pose naked. *Playgirl* said fine, but when I arrived for the shoot they changed their tune. The photographer, a guy, said, "just take it all off." I said, "Look, man, I don't get naked." He quieted down, took a couple more shots, then told me to take it off again. Again I told him no. This went on most of the day. But no, I never posed naked.

When my mom saw the layout, she didn't think it was all that bad, which kind of surprised me. But when she glanced through the rest of the issue, she nearly fainted.

As you can imagine, my teammates thought it was the greatest thing in the world—it gave them perfect ammunition. At a team meeting one day, two of the guys got up in front of the room and said there was something they felt everyone on the team should see. I had no idea what they were talking about until they opened up the *Playgirl* and showed the entire team. They started reading my quotes out loud, nailing me directly to the wall, and the whole team cracked up. I admit it was funny, but I don't think I've ever been so embarrassed in my life.

were saying that I was nothing more than "an average back." That without my offensive line I'd be just another runner.

Now it was *my* turn to get angry.

I'm the biggest fan in the world of the Los Angeles Rams' offensive line. They're not just my teammates, they're my friends. These guys break their backs and they barely get recognition. And everything I've achieved so far in the NFL I owe

It's hard to tell in this shot, but I've just gotten a block from one of our offensive linemen. I've got tremendous respect for the Rams' offensive line. It's one of the best in football.

Stu Nahan, a local TV reporter, looking for some quotes. In the old days dealing with the press was an afterthought for athletes. Today it's very much a part of the sport.

in part to their hard work. That's not just lip service. I mean that.

But that wasn't the point here. By acknowledging the importance of our offensive line, the Oilers were totally correct. What bothered me was the crack that I was an average back. I've got my share of faults, but a runaway ego isn't one of them. When people ask me how I rate myself against the game's best backs, I

Closing in on O.J.

I wear a lot of pads when I play football—always have. I don't like to get injured. The Rams don't pay me to watch.

Signing autographs is one thing, but one time a fan ran up to me and kissed me on the neck. A male fan. That was going a little too far.

I'm trying to throw a stiff arm. Stiff arms are a running back's weapon. They not only stun the defender, they can buy a few extra yards.

tell them I feel like I'm *one* of the best—not the best, but one of them. On the other hand, I definitely don't think of myself as average.

The more I thought about it the madder I got. Coming from another team, another city, it might not have bothered me quite so much. But this was the place where I grew up. I felt the Oilers were out to embarrass me.

I've never believed in fighting with other teams through the press. Everything gets settled on Sunday anyway—why waste your breath? So I didn't respond to the Oilers' remarks.

Inside I wasn't so cool.

The Oilers were playing dirty football. I take that back— **some** *of the Oilers were playing clean. But some of them weren't. Those Oilers were twisting my neck and ankles, hitting me after the whistle, diving onto pile-ups. It was turning into a war.*

It was a violent game. And very, very verbal. Things got nastier as the game went on. Talking led to pushing and pushing led to flat-out fights. I don't want to make them out to be the villains here, but the Oilers were playing dirty football. I take that back—*some* of the Oilers were playing clean. But some of them weren't. Those Oilers were twisting my neck and ankles, hitting me after the whistle, diving onto pile-ups. It was turning into a war.

In the final quarter, as if the game wasn't wild enough, the Oilers were fired up over something else: I was closing in on the all-time, single-season rushing record. The Oilers were determined not to let me break it. Not against them, not on a day like this.

Let me insert a little background at this point. In 1973, playing for the Buffalo Bills, O. J. Simpson had the most prolific season of any runner in NFL history. Although the season was only 14 games long back then (as opposed to 16 now), O.J. ran for 2,003 yards. As I began my second season, the record still belonged to O.J.

After my rookie year, I had gone into 1984 with high expectations. But again I surprised even myself. As the season unwound,

Closing in on O.J.

It's a great feeling when you get this much daylight.

The Pro Bowl is played every January in Hawaii. It's a great honor to be selected. And Hawaii's not real shabby either.

I found myself in pursuit of O.J.'s record. Even to approach that kind of record, everything has got to go just right. That season it did. Coach Robinson was a firm believer in the running game. Already outstanding, our blocking became sensational when we acquired David Hill, maybe the best-blocking tight end in football. I was finding the holes and breaking tackles. For a team that likes to run, it was a dream season.

As our numbers on the ground began to pile up, I kept hearing my name mentioned along with O.J.'s. I can't tell you how great that made me feel. When I was a kid I had two special heroes: John Wayne and O. J. Simpson. I was an O.J. fanatic. When I was in high school, at first I wanted number 32 so I could be just like the Juice. I remember the day the coaches issued jerseys. I had one in each hand—number 32 and number 19. At the last minute I took 19 because I wanted to be different, to do my own thing. But I never stopped admiring O.J. Not then, and not when I was chasing his record.

Getting back to the Houston game, I went into it needing 211 yards to pass the Juice. Most people figured I would pass him the next week, in our final game of the regular season, against the San Francisco 49ers. I also thought that would be a nice time to do it. Sure, it would have been great to do it against the Oilers, at home in front of our fans, but it didn't seem realistic. Two hundred eleven yards in one game definitely qualified as a long shot. Besides, the game against the 49ers would be on national TV—all my friends and family back home would get to see it. To make the whole picture complete, O.J. would be calling it for ABC from up in the booth.

My feelings changed in the middle of the Oiler game. We were rolling up yardage, for one thing. For another, the Oilers were starting to get on my nerves. The hell with San Francisco. I wanted to break the record on the Oilers.

Our offensive linemen wanted the record then, too. Because the Oilers had made a big mistake: they started talking garbage to our offensive linemen. Trying to intimidate me is one thing; it'll get me hot, but I'm not going to fight you over it. Trying to

O. J. Simpson was one of my heroes when I was a kid. I wasn't disappointed when I met him in person—he's a real classy guy.

intimidate our offensive linemen borders on masochism. On a football field, those guys will fight in a second. We had David Hill, Jackie Slater, Bill Bain, Kent Hill, Dennis Harrah, Irv Pankey, and

Doug Smith. You're going to intimidate guys like that? Good luck, I hope you've got lots of insurance.

The Oilers aren't exactly sissies, though, and they definitely gave it their best shot. If we were going to break the record on them, they had no intention of making it easy for us. In fact, once we got close, they actually started talking about it at the line of scrimmage. Let's just say they weren't wishing me luck.

It was more like: "Hey, you four-eyed bleep, you aren't getting any records off of us."

But the Oilers couldn't stop us. With 9:14 left in the game, I swept around end for 32 yards. That put me at 1,984 yards, only 27 behind O.J. Things were getting interesting.

At 5:49 I scored on a six-yard touchdown. That gave us a 27–16 lead, which would eventually be the final score. Then the word came from the sideline: I had 1,998 yards, just five short of O.J. But now Houston had the ball. If they could kill the clock, we'd be forced to wait until next week. To tell you the truth, I wasn't real worried about it. The game was ours and we were right in the race for the playoffs. That was the bottom line. Still, to get that close....

Houston was driving. Then, with 3:30 left, Warren Moon dropped back to pass. He threw a bomb to our goal line. Vince Newsome leaped in and intercepted. Vince ran the ball all the way back to our 31-yard line. The offense practically raced back on the field. This was it.

As long as I live, I'll never forget the feeling in that huddle. It was absolutely electric. I don't recall exactly what was said, or even if the record was mentioned. But nobody had to mention it—their eyes all told the story. We were five yards away from making history.

As soon as I heard the call, I sensed we would break the record that play. Jeff Kemp, our quarterback, called a 47-Gap. Every offense has its bread and butter and the 47-Gap was ours. It was always run the same way. I would line up five yards behind Jeff. On the snap of the ball I would take a jab step, just a fake, toward the left. Then I would cut back right, off the tackle, where Jeff would pitch me the ball. We'd been hurting people with it all day and all season. I had a feeling we would again.

I dug into my stance. When Jeff got the snap, first I took my jab step, then I veered right. As I got the pitch I moved toward the hole. It was plowed wide open—Kent Hill and Bill Bain had blown their men off the line. I broke into the Oiler backfield. A couple of them got a piece of me, but their hands slid down my shirt. Greg Bingham finally wrestled me down.

It was a nine-yard gain—the record was ours! It gave me 215 for the ball game, 2,007 for the season. After 98 more yards in the 49ers game, I would end the season with 2,105—a new NFL record.

Even after the season ended, after we lost to the New York Giants in the playoffs, the glow from my record still hadn't faded. We were bitterly disappointed that we hadn't made it to the Super Bowl. But we had broken O.J.'s record as a team, an accomplishment shared together. It was a tremendous thrill, a once-in-a-lifetime feeling.

6
ONE WIN FROM THE SUPER BOWL

I never thought of myself as a holdout.

But that's precisely what I became in the summer of 1985. By then my new agents were Ken Norton, the former heavyweight champion, and Jack Rodri, his business manager. Jim Murray, the respected columnist for the *Los Angeles Times*, wrote a tongue-in-check column about what a great agent Ken would be. Who in their right mind, Murray wrote, would want to mess with him? That's not what I had in mind when I signed with Kenny and Jack, but I was aware that they were fairminded yet tough negotiators. It turned out I would need them.

My holdout lasted 47 days, right through training camp and two games into the regular season. I don't want to dwell too long here on my holdout, because the contract I eventually signed with the Rams later that season was a fair one. I do want to say that I was not trying to hurt the Rams or their fans. It was strictly a business decision, just as other people sometimes have to make business decisions when dealing with their bosses. The *Times'* Jim Murray summed it up pretty well:

DICKERSON'S RANGERS

I'm still young myself, only 26 years old, and I love working with children. Especially in L.A., where I make my home, I feel it's important to be part of the community. This past spring, I got involved in Dickerson's Rangers, a local chapter of the Just Say No to Drugs program. With Mayor Tom Bradley and the Department of Parks and Recreation, I work with 30 different clubs across Los Angeles, with children 6 to 17 years old. What we basically do is this: get together in a park, have some fun, and then talk about the harmful effects of using drugs. The kids get a chance to get some things off their chests, I get a chance to tell them that drugs are a dead-end street. When you become a Ranger, you get a T-shirt, a cap, and an official membership card. We do it in the spring when the football season is over, so there's plenty of time to sign up.

If you're interested in becoming a Ranger or you know of someone who might be interested, you can call these numbers: in the San Fernando Valley region, call 818-989-8616; in the metropolitan region, call 213-485-4876; and in the Pacific region (west side and beaches), call 213-837-8116.

"Eric Dickerson, who last year ran for more yards in a single season than any back in NFL history, is unhappy with a contract signed when he was a mere collegian—it calls for somewhere around $350,000 a year, the kind of wages you give punt returners or backup quarterbacks."

In a nutshell, that's the way I felt. Considering what I had achieved my first two years in the league; considering the wear and tear that the Rams' offense puts on a runner's body; considering that the average career in the NFL is 4.3 years (even less for a runner); considering what other runners were earning,

That's us—Dickerson's Rangers—a local offshoot of Nancy Reagan's Just Say No to Drugs Program. It's doing a lot of good around Los Angeles.

runners who had accomplished less than I had, I sincerely felt I was entitled to a raise.

Football players definitely make a great living, but most people

Mayor Tom Bradley is also a part of Dickerson's Rangers. He's active in the war against drugs.

Lighting up a child's face, with an autograph or just a hello, is something we never tire of.

All these kids wearing Eric Dickerson T-shirts? Must be an amazing coincidence. Of course I'm just kidding. That's one of the things we give to Dickerson's Rangers.

If I can help one person give up drugs, or never try them, then I've accomplished a lot.

don't realize something about NFL contracts: virtually no one in the NFL has a no-cut contract. If management wants to, it can cut a player right in the middle of the season, and then the team doesn't have to pay him another cent. Just like that, he's out on his own. When I chose to holdout, it wasn't out of greed. It was because I didn't want to wait any longer to be paid what I knew I was worth. If I waited and waited, and then an injury ended my career, where would I be? Football is the greatest game in the world, but it's also a business. You have to look out for yourself.

Football players definitely make a great living, but most people don't realize something about NFL contracts: virtually no one in the NFL has a no-cut contract. If management wants to, it can cut a player right in the middle of the season, and then the team doesn't have to pay him another cent. Just like that, he's out on his own.

I wound up with 1,234 yards and 12 touchdowns in the 1985 season. In the early part of the year there was a question buzzing around Los Angeles: did his holdout affect Eric Dickerson? I really don't think so. For a lot of backs, 1,234 yards would be an excellent season. I have to admit that for me, 1,234 is what I consider an off season. I could have played better and I'll take my share of the blame. But offense is an 11-man proposition; everything has to click to be successful. Last year there were times when we just weren't all clicking. It's no big secret that our passing game wasn't efficient. And when every team you play is keying on the run, well, it can make life difficult for a running back.

Before I move on to another subject, in case anyone is still wondering, my disagreement with the Rams did not change my relationship with Georgia Frontiere, our owner. Georgia has always been good to me; she's done a lot of nice things for me

I'm used to being surrounded, but usually it's on Sundays in the fall. And the people are much bigger.

and my family. People wonder if Georgia is popular with the players. I can assure you she is. I mean, we don't sit around and talk about it all the time, but I can tell by the way people react when she's around them that they really seem to like her and feel comfortable with her. Some owners don't have much contact with their players, but that's not the case with Georgia. She'll walk down on the field and wish everyone a good game, or ask them how they're feeling. One thing in particular impressed me a lot: she doesn't spend time just with the team's stars. She'll talk to players she hardly knows, guys who rarely play or guys who are only on the team at minicamp. Georgia's a fine person. She's also a good owner. I enjoy working for her.

People wonder if Georgia Frontiere is popular with the players. I can assure you she is. One thing in particular impressed me a lot: she doesn't spend time just with the team's stars. She'll talk to players she hardly knows, guys who rarely play or guys who are only on the team at minicamp.

RUNNERS GET THEIR LICKS IN TOO

One of the hardest hits I ever gave out was against the Cleveland Browns. The Browns have a defensive back named Don Rogers, a graduate of UCLA. He's one of the toughest defensive backs in the league, a guy who will cut you in two. But on one play I got the best of him. It was about third and five, and we were driving for the winning touchdown. The play was a handoff to me. When I got to the hole, it was just Don and me. He moved up to fill the hole and I ran right over him. I mean *right* over him.

If nobody minds, how about if I talk about some football now? Because even if I didn't have the greatest year of my life, the Rams had a solid regular season in 1985. Some of the highlights:

- a seven-game winning streak to open the season
- with an 11–5 record, our first NFC West title since 1979
- critical wins, on the road, against defending Super Bowl champs San Francisco 49ers and the always-tough Seattle Seahawks
- eight players selected to the Pro Bowl
- the third consecutive season of improvement under Coach John Robinson.

JUST SAY NO TO DRUGS

I don't take drugs. Never even tried them, not even once, and I never will. That's one reason Nancy Reagan asked me to be a spokesperson for her "Just Say No to Drugs" program.

The fight against drugs means a lot to me. When I was a child, John Wayne was one of my heroes. If someone had told me John Wayne was doing drugs, I would have been crushed. Since athletes are heroes to today's children, I feel it's their moral responsibility to stay clean from drugs. Some people think that athletes shouldn't be held up as role models, that it isn't fair. Well, fair or not, the fact remains that we *are* looked upon as role models. And we've got to act accordingly.

I know I'm not going to influence every person who has a drug problem. But if I can help just one, that's one less person doing drugs. And that can save a person's life.

We opened the playoffs against Dallas, and once again I was right in the spotlight. How do you figure it? For a guy who's never looking for controversy, I sure manage to find my share.

I can still relate to kids and I love to help them with problems.

I'm proud of the fact that I've never taken a single drug. I'm happy and healthy without them.

I was preparing for our game against the Cowboys, minding my own business, when again I got dragged into the news by an opposing team's player. This time it was Eugene Lockhart, the Cowboys' fine middle linebacker. A few days before the game, Eugene started talking about how he couldn't stand me, stuff like that. Then he added that when he was at the University of Houston and I was at SMU, I never gained even 100 yards against them. Now, *that* I had to laugh at. When I was a junior I had something like 109 yards against Houston. And when I was a senior I had one game in which I ran for 247. I guess Eugene's memory failed him.

I was preparing for our game against the Cowboys, minding my own business, when again I got dragged into the news by an opposing team's player. This time it was Eugene Lockhart, the Cowboys' fine middle linebacker. A few days before the game Eugene started talking about how he couldn't stand me, stuff like that.

You have to understand that Eugene and I never got along, even when we were in college. Houston and SMU were bitter rivals in the Southwestern Conference, and there was a lot of bickering between the two teams' athletes. Eugene and I were no exception.

I first met Eugene my junior year. I was visiting a friend at one of Houston's dorms when Eugene walked up to me.

"They treat you *boys* good at SMU?" he wanted to know.

"We don't have boys at SMU," I said. "They treat you *boys* good at Houston?"

We went back and forth like this for a while, and finally I cut the conversation short. "Listen, I don't want to stand here and argue with you. You go to the University, I go to SMU. You boys play here, we men play there. Let's leave it at that."

I really enjoy making public appearances, but football still comes first.

One time I invited the press to change positions with me, but nobody took me up on my offer. I was obviously kidding, but I was also trying to make a point: Football isn't an easy game. Don't be so quick to criticize.

When people stop and think of number 29, I want them to think of a winner. And a good person.

We were just a couple of college kids, defending the honor of our schools, but that last remark got Eugene ticked off. Then things got worse in that game my junior year. It was a critical, emotional game—a lot of pushing, a lot of talking—and I pulled a real hot-dog move: I was breezing toward the end zone, on my way to a long touchdown run, and I started pointing at Houston's sideline. Eugene and his teammates didn't like that.

In the Houston-SMU game when I was a senior, Eugene couldn't play because he had a broken arm. I saw him on the sideline before the game.

> **ALL THE PADS IN THE WORLD WON'T PROTECT YOUR LUNGS**
>
> I'm involved with the American Lung Association, as the chairman of their Future Workers Education Project. Future Workers educates students and teachers in vocational training programs about occupational lung hazards, and about how to prevent lung disease caused by toxic substances in the workplace. It's a serious problem—statistics show that more than 65,000 Americans contract an occupational lung disease every year, and more than 25,000 Americans die from it. I'm very lucky to have been given a healthy body. One way I can give thanks is by helping other young people maintain their own health.

"Eugene," I teased him, "you don't want to play today anyway, because we're going to roll over your ass."

Eugene just stood there seething.

But that was all college stuff, stuff I thought I had left behind. Maybe I had, but Eugene clearly didn't. As I said, Eugene was letting me have it the week before the Cowboys game. Everyone wanted me to say that I hated Eugene too, but I wouldn't fall for that. I *didn't* hate Eugene, didn't even have anything against him, so why should I say I do? Besides, as I've said, I've never believed in waging war through the press. So again I kept my mouth shut and waited for the game.

I do have to admit Eugene got me mad. I remember thinking, "I am not going to let this man get the best of me." I kept those feelings mostly to myself, but I did confide in one of my buddies.

"By the third quarter," I told him, "Eugene will be helping me up."

I thought we could beat the Bears. Believe me, I didn't underestimate them for a minute. By the time we met them their record was 16–1. I'd also seen their "Super Bowl Shuffle." These guys could even carry a tune. That's when I got hit by a truck named Mike Singletary.

I was wrong—Eugene never did help me up. It didn't matter though. We were red hot, and the Rams beat the Cowboys, 20–0. Our blocking was fierce and I had one of the greatest games of my life: touchdown runs of 40 and 55 yards led to 248 yards for the day, an NFL playoff game record.

As for Eugene, he surprised me—he didn't say a single word to me the entire game. I carried the ball 31 times, though, and he and I did have some hellacious collisions. One time it was one on one, just him and me, and I planted my helmet, hard, right on his arm. Eugene's like me, he doesn't like to show that he's hurt, but I knew he was. He walked to the sideline holding his arm, and when he came back on the field he was still holding it. Hurt or not, Eugene played a very tough game. He may have done a lot of talking during the week, but when Sunday came, he backed it up.

For me, that game was one of our sweetest wins. Not only were we on our way to the NFC championship, but we got there by stomping on the Cowboys. I like to beat every team in the NFL, but if there's one team in the league that I *really* like to beat, it's the Dallas Cowboys. I guess it goes back to when I was in college,

This is Rams Park a few years ago, and I'm blocking at practice for former Ram Vince Ferragamo. Vince is now with the Green Bay Packers.

Injuries are an athlete's darkest fear. So far I've been fortunate—I've managed to stay relatively healthy.

Sometimes you play against people you're friends with. You have to forget that during the game, but afterwards it's nice to see how they're doing.

living in Dallas. I got so fed up with hearing how great the Cowboys were. Even if they were great, I was a Rams fan and didn't want to hear it. I always said that I would love to face the Cowboys and have a great game. That playoff game was my chance, and I did it.

Next came the Chicago Bears.

I thought we could beat the Bears. Believe me, I didn't underestimate them for a minute. By the time we met them their record was 16–1. While we'd been blanking the Cowboys, they'd been destroying a tough Giants team, 24–0. With its eight-man lines and blitzing fronts, their defense was driving offensive coordinators into careers selling insurance. I'd also seen their "Super Bowl Shuffle." These guys could even carry a tune.

But regardless of all that, we'd matched up well with the Bears the last two times we'd played them, beating them both times. I'd had good games too, with 127 yards in 1983 and 149 in 1984. I went into the Bears game feeling good.

I also went into it feeling cold. The game was played in

Back in Sealy where the pace is so much slower. That's me with Viola and my grandparents, Horace and Johnnie Mae Shavers.

Chicago's Soldier Field, a few blocks and a brutally icy wind from the city's lakefront. The cold didn't beat us though: the Chicago Bears did. I got a pretty good idea of what was to come early in the second quarter. That's when I got hit by a truck named Mike Singletary.

The Bears' defense talks to you a lot, as any other team's does, but they never play dirty. They play rough but they stop at the whistle.

I played against Mike when he was at Baylor, and the guy gave me more than my share of headaches. Unfortunately he hasn't changed much. He's one of the top players in the NFL, last year's Defensive Player of the Year. Anyway, I was running through what I thought was a nice hole when suddenly Singletary met me with a full head of steam. I never saw him coming and he really got me good. Right in the face with the front of his helmet. It was like my body went into shock. I'll never forget it. It was one of the hardest hits of my career.

The rest of the afternoon wasn't much more fun. With their defense stacked on the line of scrimmage, the Bears took us right out of our running game. And when you take the Los Angeles Rams out of their running game, you can pretty much do what you want. I carried the ball 17 times for only 46 yards. Everywhere I went I was smothered in black.

The final score was 24–0. I hated to lose, but I came away with tremendous respect for the Bears. Actually, I've always admired the Bears. Even when they weren't that good, they always had a lot of tough guys. Their defense talks to you a lot, as any other team does, but they never play dirty. They play rough but they stop at the whistle. I was glad when the Bears beat New England in the Super Bowl. It was nice to see Walter Payton get his ring.

Losing to the Chicago Bears in the 1985 season's playoffs was a big disappointment. But afterwards, since it couldn't be us in the Super Bowl, I was glad to see Walter Payton finally get his ring.

No one should forget about the Rams though. Last year was a super season, one game away from the Super Bowl. Who knows what can happen in 1986? As Coach Robinson said after the Bears game: "The door is right there and we're knocking on it."

I feel good about my own future. I love playing football, I'm healthy, and I'm looking forward to whatever is in front of me.

I'm ready to go.